George Gibbs

Instructions for researcerelative to the Ethnology and Philology of America

George Gibbs

Instructions for researcerelative to the Ethnology and Philology of America

ISBN/EAN: 9783741142451

Manufactured in Europe, USA, Canada, Australia, Japa

Cover: Foto ©Thomas Meinert / pixelio.de

Manufactured and distributed by brebook publishing software
(www.brebook.com)

George Gibbs

Instructions for researcerelative to the Ethnology and Philology of America

SMITHSONIAN MISCELLANEOUS COLLECTIONS.

—————— 160 ——————

INSTRUCTIONS

FOR RESEARCH RELATIVE TO THE

ETHNOLOGY AND PHILOLOGY

OF

AMERICA.

PREPARED FOR THE SMITHSONIAN INSTITUTION.

BY

GEORGE GIBBS.

WASHINGTON:
SMITHSONIAN INSTITUTION:
MARCH, 1863.

CONTENTS.

INSTRUCTIONS

RELATIVE TO THE

ETHNOLOGY AND PHILOLOGY
OF AMERICA.

INTRODUCTORY REMARKS.

THE Smithsonian Institution is desirous of extending and completing its collections of facts and materials relative to the Ethnology, Archæology, and Philology of the races of mankind inhabiting, either now or at any previous period, the continent of America, and earnestly solicits the coöperation in this object of all officers of the United States government, and travellers, or residents who may have it in their power to render any assistance.

JOSEPH HENRY,
Secretary S. I.

SMITHSONIAN INSTITUTION,
WASHINGTON, March 1, 1863.

ETHNOLOGY.

CRANIA.—Among the first of the desiderata of the Smithsonian Institution, is a full series of the skulls of American Indians. The jealousy with which they guard the remains of their friends renders such a collection in most cases a difficult task, but there are others in which these objects can be procured without offence. Numerous tribes have become extinct, or have removed from their former abodes; the victims of war are often left where they fall; and the bones of the friendless and of slaves are neglected. Where, without offence to the living, acquisitions of this kind can be made, they will be gladly received as an important contribution to our knowledge of the race.

Various methods of disposing of the dead have prevailed among different tribes, as burning, burial, deposit in caves, in lodges, beneath piles of stone, and in wooden sepulchres erected above-ground, placing on scaffolds or in canoes, and attaching to the trunks of trees. In many instances the bones, after a season, are collected together, and brought into a common cemetery. Where the first-mentioned form, that of burning, is followed, we must, of course, look to chance for the preservation of the remains. This method is, however, more rare than the others.

It is requisite, for the purpose of arriving at particular results, that the most positive determination be made of the nation or tribe to which a skull belongs. In extensive prairie countries, hunted over or traversed by various tribes, or where, as on the Pacific coast, several tribes and even stocks inhabit a district of limited extent, this is often difficult, or even impossible. Unless, therefore, information of a direct nature is obtained, the collector should be guarded in assigning absolute nationality to his specimens. It will be better to state accurately the locality whence they are derived, and the owners or frequenters of the neighborhood, to one of which they are likely to belong. Where several specimens are collected, each should be numbered to correspond with a catalogue in which the above points are mentioned; as also whether it was found in a grave or other place of deposit,

the character of the ornaments and utensils placed with it, and
whether it was in its original place or had been combined with
others. Finally, it should be ascertained whether the tomb was that
of existing or recent inhabitants of the country, or of more ancient
date,—such, for example, as the mound-builders of the Ohio; and, in
this latter case, if the remains are those of the original inhabitant,
or have been since deposited. In this inquiry the character of the
articles buried with the body will often furnish a clue. The same
precaution should be adopted where tribes have been removed from
their native regions to a different locality. In short, where any doubt
exists in the mind of the collector, all those circumstances should be
examined into which in the absence of direct testimony, will facilitate
a conclusion as to origin.

It may be mentioned in this connection, that among some nations, it
is the custom to marry out of the tribe, as a matter of policy. Skulls
of women found in the cemeteries of one of these might therefore
very probably belong to an adjoining tribe, and, possibly, to one of
an entirely different stock. In such cases, too, there can be no certainty that the men themselves are of the pure blood of one race, and
it is, therefore, important to ascertain if this custom exists. Among
those tribes where flattening or altering the head is common to both
sexes, particular suspicion should attach to any having the skull unaltered. This process is usually a mark of rank, or at least of freedom,
and an unaltered skull, if found in a burial-place or well-marked receptacle, may almost be assumed to be that of a stranger; if neglected,
it is probably that of a slave. But as slaves were often buried with their
owners, even this is not a positive conclusion. Among some of the
Pacific tribes, however, compression of the head is confined to females,
or is, at any rate, only carried to any considerable extent among them.
Slaves are sometimes of the same tribe with their owners, but they are
more frequently purchased from others; and it should be noted that
on the Pacific the course of the trade has been from south to north.

In order to ascertain whether differences of form exist among different stocks, the accumulation of as many specimens as possible of
each tribe is desirable, and duplicates moreover afford the means of
extending the collection by exchange.

Skulls which have been altered in shape possess a certain interest
in themselves, though they are in other respects disadvantageous
for comparison. The practice, in different forms, formerly existed
more widely than at present, several tribes in the southern States, as
the Natchez, &c., having been addicted to it. Two methods are still

employed in North America: that of flattening the head by pressure on the forehead, as practised among the Chinooks and other tribes in Oregon and Washington Territory, and that of elongating it, peculiar to a few on the northern end of Vancouver Island.

SPECIMENS OF ART, ETC.—Another department to which the Institution wishes to direct the attention of collectors, is that of the weapons, implements, and utensils, the various manufactures, ornaments, dresses, &c., of the Indian tribes.

Such a collection may naturally be arranged under three periods. The first, that of the races which had already passed away before the discovery of the continent by Europeans, or whose extinction may be considered as coeval with that event; next, of the tribes who have disappeared with the settlement of the Atlantic States and the country between the Alleghanies and the Mississippi; and finally, that of the present time, or that of the yet existing nations, confined to the northern and western portions of the continent and to Mexico.

It is among the last that the greatest variety exists, and of which it is especially important to make immediate collections, as many articles are of a perishable nature, and the tribes themselves are passing away or exchanging their own manufactures for those of the white race. It is hardly necessary to specify any as of particular interest, for almost every thing has its value in giving completeness to a collection. Among the most noticeable, however, are dresses and ornaments, bows and arrows, lances, war-clubs, knives, and weapons of all kinds, saddles with their furniture, models of lodges, parflech packing covers and bags, cradles, mats, baskets of all sorts, gambling implements, models of canoes (as nearly as possible in their true proportions), paddles, fish-hooks and nets, fish-spears and gigs, pottery, pipes, the carvings in wood and stone of the Pacific coast Indians, and the wax and clay models of those of Mexico, tools used in dressing skins and in other manufactures, metates or stone mortars, &c., &c.

In making these collections, care should be taken to specify the tribes from which they are obtained, and where any doubt may exist, the particular use to which each is applied. Thus, for instance, among the Californians, one form of basket is used for holding water; another for sweeping the seeds from various plants and grasses; a third, as their receptacle during the process of collection; a fourth, for storage; still another, in which to pound the seeds; again, one to boil the porridge made from the flour; and finally, others as dishes from which the preparation is eaten. It will also be desirable to ascertain the Indian names given to each article.

Of the second class, the remains are also numerous, and are scattered through all the States east of the Mississippi, in the form of axes, arrow-heads, sinkers for nets, fleshing chisels, and other implements of stone, and in some cases fragments of rude pottery.

To the first class belong the only *antiquities* of America, and these are of various descriptions. They include the tools found in the northern copper-mines; the articles inclosed in the mounds of Ohio and elsewhere; the images common in Kentucky and Tennessee, indicating, among other things, the worship of the Phallus; pottery, the fragments of which are abundant in Florida, the Gulf States, and on the Gila, connecting an extinct with an existing art; and especially those specimens frequently disinterred in the Mexican States, belonging to the era of Aztec or Toltecan civilization. It is especially important to ascertain the antiquity of these by careful observation of the circumstances under which they are discovered, in order not to confound ancient with modern utensils.

To this class also belong those articles found under conditions which connect archæology with geology, and which may be classed as follows:

1. The contents of shell beds of ancient date found on the sea-coasts and bays, often deeply covered with soil and overgrown with trees; among which, besides the shells themselves, implements of stone, bones of fish, animals, and birds used for food, are frequently met with. The examination of these collections in Denmark and other countries of northern Europe has led to the discovery of remains belonging to a period when a people having no other implements than those of stone or bone occupied the coast prior to the settlement there of the present race. It is possible that a similar investigation in America may carry us back to a very remote period in aboriginal history.

2. Human remains, or implements of human manufacture, bones of animals bearing the marks of tools or of subjection to fire, found in caves beneath deposits of earth, and more especially of stalagmite or stony material formed by droppings from the roof.

3. Spear and arrow heads, or other weapons, and evidences of fire discovered in connection with bones of extinct animals, such as the mammoth, fossil elephant, &c., among superficial deposits, such as salt-licks, &c.

4. Implements of the same description found in deposits of sand and gravel, or other like material, exposed in bluffs or steep banks, such as have recently attracted the attention of European geologists.

In all these cases the utmost care should be taken to ascertain with absolute certainty the true relations of these objects. In the case of the shell-banks, the largest trees, where any exist, should, if practicable, be cut down and the annual rings counted. Next, the depth of the superincumbent deposit of earth should be measured, and its character noted, whether of gravel, sand, or decomposed vegetable matter; as also whether it has been stratified by the action of water. Next, the thickness of the shell-bed should be ascertained, and the height of its base above present high-water mark; as also whether it exhibit any marks of stratification. Finally, the face of the bed having been uncovered, a thorough examination should be made, commencing at the top and carefully preserving all objects which exhibits signs of human art, and noting the depth in the deposit at which they were discovered. Specimens of each species of shell should be collected, and all bones or fragments of them saved. Evidences of the use of fire should be watched for and recorded.

In the search of caverns, the same system should be followed. First, the floor should be inspected for any recent remains either of men or animals; next, the superficial earth should be carefully removed over a considerable space and thoroughly examined at various depths, the results, if any, being kept separate, and marked accordingly. Where a stalagmitic deposit, such as is common in limestone caverns, forms the floor, it must be broken up and its thickness measured. The underlying materials should then be cautiously removed and sorted over, each layer being kept by itself; and where any remains are discovered, the utmost precaution should be taken to determine their actual circumstances. If, for instance, they are bones of men, it should be ascertained whether the skeleton is entire and in a natural position, indicative of having been buried there, or scattered, as also its position relative to any other remains, whether under or over them; if of animals, whether they exhibit the marks of tools, and above all, evidences of the employment of fire. Every fragment of bone or other evidence of animal life should be preserved and marked with the order of its succession in depth.

The same precautions should be taken in the other cases mentioned, the conditions under which the objects are found, and the depth and character of covering of each being noted, and full sets of specimens sent for examination.

Besides collecting the articles heretofore mentioned, persons able to make the investigations, are invited to report the information sought in the following paper prepared by the late Prof. W. W. Turner.

Hints for Ethnological Inquiry.

Inquiries of this description have the two-fold object of ascertaining the present condition of these tribes and their past history. Although both branches of the investigation have of course a mutual bearing upon each other, yet the former has more of a practical, the latter more of a scientific character; the former is comparatively easy, the latter environed with difficulties. In examining into the numbers, physical and mental characteristics, and actual condition of the Indian tribes, we are accumulating data for beneficent, legislative, and philanthropic action in their behalf. The work, moreover, is a mere matter of observation, to be accomplished with the requisite expenditure of time and labor to almost any degree of minute accuracy that may be desired. On the contrary, any reliable knowledge of ante-Columbian events, that is now attainable, can, from the nature of things, be only general in its character, and the fruit of laborious induction from the comparison of many diverse particulars. As none of the tribes of this continent, not even the most advanced, ever arrived at the grand and fruitful idea of an alphabetic character for commemorating their thoughts and deeds, almost their entire history previous to the advent of Europeans is left a mysterious blank. To ascertain, if possible, the origin of the aboriginal population of this portion of our globe, to trace the migrations and conquests of the various nations that composed it from one part of the continent to another, to disclose their superstitions, their manners and customs, their knowledge of the arts of war and peace—in short, to place before us a moving panorama of America in the olden time—such is the purpose which the scientific ethnologist has in view, and to accomplish which he neglects no source of information that promises to cast even a single ray of light into the obscurity with which the subject is surrounded.

Names of tribes.—In addition to the name by which a tribe calls itself, it is desirable to ascertain those which are given to it by surrounding tribes, together with the literal meaning of each name.

Geographical position.—Give as accurately as may be the size of the territory, whether mainland or island, belonging to each tribe; its climate, soil, and general character; also its animal, vegetable, and mineral productions.

Number.—What is the number of individuals in the tribe? State, if you can, the number of adult males, females, and children respontively. Has the number of the tribe increased or diminished to any remarkable extent; and if so, to what cause is the change owing?

Physical constitution.—It is essential to notice the general stature of the people, the form of their bodies generally, and the proportions of their limbs; the form of the skull and the facial angle; the features; have them any thing which distinguishes them from other people? What are the color and texture of their skin and hair? What beard have they? What is the color of their eyes? Are they generally handsome or ugly? Have they much or but little muscular strength? Are they remarkable for the peculiar perfection of any of their organs, as that of sight, of hearing, of smelling; or for any corporeal faculties, as speed in running, facility of climbing, of diving and remaining long under water, or for nimbleness and dexterity, or the reverse? What is the ordinary duration of life among them? It is highly desirable, also, that photographs should be taken of individuals of each tribe.

Picture-writing, etc.—A full description is desirable of any modes that the natives may practise of recording events or communicating ideas by sensible signs, especially paintings or picture-writings, however rude, whether on pieces of bark or skin, on their dwellings or implements, on rocks, &c. When the object itself containing the record cannot be secured and brought away, exact drawings of the figures should be taken, colored after the originals. Every circumstance respecting the locality and people among whom found should be noted down, together with the interpretations of the natives (endeavoring in all cases to have the independent testimony of more than one), when attainable.

Dress.—State the materials, colors, and fashion of their dresses and ornaments. Do they paint themselves; and if so, with what materials? Do they paint variously on different occasions, as on festivals and before going to war? Give specimens of the figures they employ, especially of any that may be distinctive of the tribe or band. The same of tattooing, if practised. Some tribes of the northwest make large incisions in the under lip, others flatten the heads of their infants by compression; all such things should be observed and accurately noted respecting each tribe.

Food.—Describe the materials of which it consists, with the mode of procuring it, as by hunting, fishing, collecting roots, berries, &c. Do they practise agriculture at all; if so, to what extent; and what grains, roots, etc., do they cultivate? Do they rear any domestic animals? Do they make any stimulating drinks of their own; and are they fond of tobacco or any other narcotic?

Dwellings.—Are these permanent or movable; of what materials are they constructed, and how? Are they entirely above or partially under ground; what is their interior arrangement? Drawings of both exteriors and interiors should be made, so as to give an accurate idea of their peculiarities. On whom does the labor of construction fall, the men or the women; and in case of migration, is the entire structure removed, or only the outside covering? When a number of dwellings are placed near each other, as when a tribe encamp together on a spot, is any regular mode of arrangement observed? Have they any buildings set apart for public purposes, as business, amusement, or worship; and how are they constructed?

Arts.—An exceedingly interesting branch of inquiry, and one too often overlooked or but imperfectly attended to by travellers, is presented to us in the primitive industrial arts of the aborigines. Of what materials is the pottery composed; is any of it turned on a wheel; how are the materials compounded; is the ware burned completely or partially; is it glazed or not? How is it ornamented? Have they any utensils of stone; and if so, what is the material? Of what materials are their arrow and spear heads manufactured, and what is the process? Are there individuals whose business it is to make them? Do they make any articles of metal; and if so, of what metals, and what is their mode of working them? How and by what means do they produce fire? Their modes of spinning, weaving, and dyeing, and the materials and implements used, are of great interest. What are their modes of trapping animals and taking fish; and how are their implements for these purposes constructed? Do they still retain the bow and arrow, or have they wholly or partially abandoned them for the use of firearms? The construction and mode of using all their implements should be described, and complete collections made of them. Their performances, too, in the way of what may be called the fine arts, merit attention; such as their drawings and paintings on smooth rocks or the barks of trees, or their vessels, their dwellings, etc.; and their carvings in wood and stone, as on pipe-bowls, paddles, bows, etc., etc. If native melodies should be discovered among them, they should by all means be noted down, together with the words sung with them.

Trade.—Do they carry on any traffic with each other, or with the whites? If so, of what articles does it consist, and how is it conducted? Have they any common standard of value which approaches the nature of money?

Religion.—What is the nature of their religious belief, as far as it

can be ascertained? What are the objects of their worship? Have
they any idea of a Creator of all things; and do they give any account
of the creation? Do they worship the sun, fire, or the serpent? What
becomes of men and animals after death? Are there any persons of
the character of priests set apart for the performance of religious ceremonies? If so, how are they supported, and in what general estimation are they held? Have they a sacred fire, and is it kept per-
petually burning?

Government.—Is the tribe commanded by the same chief or chiefs
in peace and in war, or by different ones? What is the extent of a
chief's authority; and how does he acquire it, by birth or by the choice
of the people? What are the insignia of his office, and what his
privileges? Who are entitled to speak in the councils of the tribe?
What laws have they; for instance, what are the punishments for
theft, for adultery, for murder; and by whom are punishments inflict-
ed?

Social life.—Is slavery known among them? Is female chastity
prized? What is the treatment of women by their husbands; of
children by their parents? What is the division of labor between
husband and wife? What festivals have they? enumerate them by
their native names, and describe their import, and the manner in
which they are celebrated. What ceremonies do they observe at
births, marriages, and funerals? Are women obliged to live apart
during their monthly terms, or after giving birth to a child? At what
age do marriages take place, and what degrees of consanguinity are
prohibited? May a man marry into the same band or tribe to which
he belongs, or must he go to another for a wife? Do children belong
to the tribe of the father or of the mother? Is polygamy practised?
Do the several wives stand on a footing of equality, or is one superior
to the rest; and if so, why? How is the body disposed of after death;
and what articles, if any, are buried with it?

War.—Do the warriors array themselves in a peculiar attire and
join in the war-dance before setting out? What are their weapons?
What is their treatment of captives, especially if females? Do they
practise scalping, and shave their own heads, all but the scalp-lock?

Medicine.—Are there any persons in the tribe whose profession it
is to practise the cure of diseases, or is this a part of the business of
the priest, or so-called "medicine-man?" What is their mode of
treating the principal complaints? Do they practise blood-letting,
tooth-pulling, or any other surgical operations? What plants do they
use as remedies, and for what complaints is each one applied? It is

hardly necessary to say that collections of such plants and their seeds should be made for cultivation and experiment at home.

Literature.—Have they any thing partaking of the nature of a literature among them; that is, have they any songs, tales, fables, and especially any historical legends? If they have, an endeavor should be made to record and preserve them; not so much for the information they may directly convey, as for the insight they must necessarily afford into the mental idiosyncrasy of the people. If there is any one capable of writing the language, it is much to be wished that these things should be set down in the original words, as well as an English translation.

If the Indians, like many tribes in the older States, use pictorial images for the purpose of recalling to memory the themes and general tenor of their songs, &c., specimens should be collected and delineated, and accompanied by copies of the documents they are intended to illustrate.

Calendar and Astronomy.—What divisions of time are in use among the Indians? How many days do they reckon to a month, and how many months to the year? What names are given to these days, and to the months; and what are the literal meanings of the names? Have they any length of the natural year? What names do they give to individual stars and constellations, particularly to those of the zodiac; and how do they account for eclipses? How do they ascertain and name the points of the compass? Have they any theory respecting the nature and motions of the stars, and respecting the causes of wind, rain, hail, snow, thunder, &c.?

History.—Have the tribe, as far as their knowledge extends, always lived on their present territory; if not, from what direction did they come, and to what other tribes do they state themselves to be related? What changes have been introduced among them by intercourse with the whites? With what tribes have they been, and are they now, at war? Give the name of their principal chief, and of any other eminent men among them, and of their predecessors, as far as they are remembered.

Antiquities.—Earthworks, of various forms and dimensions, and for various purposes, as for defence against enemies, for watch-towers, for funeral monuments, have been found in great numbers in the valley of the Mississippi and elsewhere; and an examination of their structure and contents has disclosed a variety of the most interesting facts respecting the races that erected them. If time and opportunity be afforded of properly examining one of them, it is highly desirable that

19 ETHNOLOGY.

it should be done. When a mound is opened, every particular respect
ing its position, size, form, and structure, should be noted down on the
spot, the description being assisted by drawings of the ground-plan
and elevation; and an accurate list should be taken of all the articles
found in it. Such as are taken should be properly labelled, and kept
by themselves, with the same care that is observed with respect to
objects of natural history. When, however, the work cannot be
thoroughly done, it is better to leave the mound unopened for a more
favorable opportunity.

PHILOLOGY.

In view of the importance of a uniform system in collecting words of the various Indian languages of North America, adapted to the use of officers of the government, travellers, and others, the following is recommended as a STANDARD VOCABULARY. It is mainly the one prepared by the late Hon. Albert Gallatin, with a few changes made by Mr. Hale, the Ethnologist of the United States Exploring Expedition, and is adopted as that upon which nearly all the collections hitherto made for the purpose of comparison have been based. For the purpose of ascertaining the more obvious relations between the various members of existing families, this number is deemed sufficient. The remote affinities must be sought in a wider research, demanding a degree of acquaintance with their languages beyond the reach of transient visitors.

The languages spoken within the limits of the United States, in which the greatest deficiencies exist, are those of the tribes comprised in the States of California and Texas, and the Territories of Utah, Nevada, and New Mexico, and to these attention is particularly directed. It is not intended, however, to confine the collection to the languages of the United States. Those of British and Russian America and of Mexico, particularly the western coast, fall within the purpose of this circular; and the alphabet may, in fact, with certain local adaptations, be used in any region.

Some of the words contained in it will of course be found inapplicable in particular sections of the country; as, for example, ice, salmon, and sturgeon among the southern tribes, buffalo among the coast tribes of the Pacific, and each should at once be omitted.

Where several languages are obtained by the same person in one district, the inquirer may substitute for these the names of familiar things, taking care that the same are carried through them all, and that they are those of native and not imported objects. Such words as coat, hat, etc., are of course useless for purposes of comparison, unless it is explained that they refer to the dress of deer-skin, the hat of basket-work used by the natives, and of their own primitive manufacture.

As the languages of savage nations, being unwritten and without fixed standard, are subject to constant change, the number of dialects is everywhere considerable. The collector is therefore recommended to obtain vocabularies in each dialect; and for the greater certainty, to employ one of those already collected, on the correctness of which reliance can be placed, as the medium of obtaining others.

Whenever leisure and opportunity offer for the collection of larger vocabularies than that here given, it will of course be desirable to procure them; as also information concerning the grammatical structure of the language, such as the modes of forming the plurals in nouns and adjectives, their declension, the conjugation of verbs, the character and use of pronouns, the number and employment of adverbs, prepositions, &c. Grammars and dictionaries, never yet published, were made of many of the languages of Upper and Lower California and the Mexican States by the Spanish missionaries, and the Smithsonian Institution has been favored with the loan of several manuscripts which are in the course of publication. It is desired to procure others, or copies of them, whenever it is possible, from all parts of both the American continents, or of printed works on the same subject. The present form is issued for the use of travellers or merely transient residents among tribes where no such records are procurable.

In making collections, the utmost care is requisite to represent accurately the sounds of unfamiliar languages, particularly those which to us appear uncouth; and the inquirer should satisfy himself, by repetition of the words to other individuals, that he has correctly acquired their pronunciation. While the assistance of interpreters conversant with the language is desirable to insure a correct understanding, the words themselves should be taken down from the lips of an Indian of the tribe. A great difference indeed exists among Indians in the purity with which they speak their own language, chiefs and men of note and women of good standing, as a general thing, speaking more correctly than common persons. Great patience is necessary to secure accuracy, as their attention soon becomes fatigued by being kept on the stretch. Whenever this is observed to be the case, it is best to postpone the subject for a time, if possible.

The character of the Indian mind is so essentially different from that of the white man, they think in so different a manner, that many precautions are necessary to avoid giving them wrong impressions of our meaning, and of course obtaining incorrect replies.

Indians not only distinguish by different names the degrees and

modifications of relationship, such as the elder from the younger
brother and sister, but women use different words from men in ad-
dressing their relations; as, for instance, a man employs one word in
saying "my father," and a woman another. Again, different words
are, at least in some languages, used in speaking of one's parents from
those used in speaking to them. It is, therefore, necessary either to
give each form, or to specify by what sex and in what sense the words
are used. Further to prevent uncertainty, it is preferable to employ
the possessive pronoun in connection with the word, as given in the
vocabulary, e. g., "my father," &c.; and this is, in fact, in consonance
with Indian practice.

Their languages are deficient in generic terms, or those representing
classes of objects. Thus very few possess words equivalent to "tree,"
"bird," "fish," &c., though names will be found for every particular
species, as each kind of oak and pine, of duck or salmon; and of certain animals, such as deer, there will be found, besides the specific
name, black or white-tailed deer, as the case may be, separate words
signifying buck, doe, and fawn, as with us. It is, therefore, essential
in obtaining such names, to ascertain definitively the object intended,
and to note this in the vocabulary.

This tendency to particularize extends to almost every class of objects. In regard to parts of the body, it has been found that in many
languages there is no one word for arm or leg, but separate ones for
the upper arm, and that below the elbow; for the thigh, and that part
below the knee. Even of the hands and feet there are often no names
embracing the whole. So, too, the words "leaf," "bark," are represented by distinct names, according to their character, as broad and
needle-shaped leaves, the woody and fibrous barks. Sheath and pocket
knives and the various forms of canoes have in like manner each their
specific names.

In respect to particular words, the following points may be noted:

Man. This must be carefully distinguished from the word "person," the collective of which is "people," i. e., Indians.

Boy, Girl, Infant. The answer often given for these is simply
"little man," "little woman," "little one."

Husband and *wife.* Distinct words exist in most languages for
these relationships; in others, it would seem as if there was only "my
man," "my woman."

Indians, people. Care must be taken that the name of the tribe is
not given unless really so designated.

Head. A very common mistake to be guarded against is the substitution of hair or scalp.

Face. The name for the forehead or eyes is, in some cases, employed for the whole face.

Neck. Throat is apt to be given instead of neck.

In naming parts of the body, as well as relationship, it will be found a very common practice with Indians to prefix the pronoun "my" to each one, as "my head," &c. The recurrence of the same syllable at the beginning of each word will indicate this.

Town, village. Generally speaking, the same word is given as for house, or it is rendered "many houses." In New Mexico, *pueblo* would have a different meaning from the habitations of the wild tribes.

Warrior. Among the tribes of the Pacific coast, where there is no distinctive class of warriors, this is frequently rendered "strong man," "quarrelsome," &c.

Friend is a word of very indefinite meaning. Instead of it, "cousin," or "one liked," will often be given.

Sun and *moon.* Curiously enough, these, among several tribes, bear the same name and are actually supposed to be the same. Others use for moon "night sun."

The Seasons. These words have been retained, though it is questionable if they have a very definite signification with Indians. The names of particular months, or "moons," warm or cold weather, or the periods in which particular occupations are followed probably, in most cases, replace them.

River, lake. For these simply the word "water" will often be given, as, among tribes of limited range, their own river or lake is "the water" which they best know.

Mountain. "Rock" is frequently the translation. Some tribes, again, apply a special name to snow peaks.

The colors. The idea of color seems to be indistinct, dark blue and dark green having, in many languages, the same name as b'ack, and yellow the same as light green.

Old and *young.* Care should be taken that the words for "old man," "young man," are not supplied; or, on the other hand, "worn out," and "new," as is often the case.

Alive is frequently rendered "not dead."

Cold, warm. Here, again, caution is requisite, as cold or warm *weather* may be given instead.

Yesterday and *to-morrow.* In some languages, a single word is used for both, the distinction being made only by the connection.

Numerals. Many tribes go no farther in counting than ten, and among those of California, it is said, some have no names for numbers beyond five. Others, on the contrary, have different sets of numerals, or rather their numerals have different terminations, one class being used in ordinary counting, the other applying to men, money, &c.

Pronouns. The personal pronouns are of two classes, one simple or absolute, the other variously called fragmentary and copulative. These last are used only in composition, as in the form of prefixes and suffixes to the verb.

Verbs. It is a matter of dispute whether the Indian verb has any true infinitive mood, as "to go," "to eat," &c., and its simplest form appears to be, in all cases, the third person singular present, "he goes," "he eats." It will be better, therefore, to obtain either this form or that of the first person, "I go," &c. The last will be found often to be combined with the copulative pronoun.

ORTHOGRAPHY.

It is, of course, essential to the proper understanding by others of the words collected, especially in view of general comparisons, that a precise and fixed system of spelling should be used, and this is more so where the usual language of the collector is English than where French or Spanish, as there is far less certainty in the pronunciation of the first than of these last. In English, for instance, four different sounds are given as belonging to the letter *a*, viz.: those in *far, fall, fat, fate*. As regards the simple vowels, the difficulty can be partly remedied by employing the Spanish or Italian sounds, as given below, and a further advantage will be found in separating the words into syllables and marking the principal one with an accent, thus. Da-ko'-ta. There are, however, in every language, sounds peculiar to itself, and the different Indian tongues abound in them, many being almost beyond our capacity to imitate and certainly to write, without some addition to the ordinary alphabet. Various systems, contemplating a universal alphabet, or one applicable to all languages, have been devised, each having its peculiar merits; but the great difficulty, never fully overcome, has been to represent intelligibly such unfamiliar sounds without confusing the inquirer with new characters or numerous marks, or, again, by employing several letters to represent a single sound. The alphabet here recommended for adoption, without pretending to remedy these defects, will at least prove an assistance to the collector in the field. Should it be necessary to represent other sounds, not included below, it will be better for him to adopt some arbitrary mark of his own, describing fully its value or meaning.

VOWELS.

A   as long in *father*, and short in German *hat* (nearly as in English *what*).

E   as long in *they* ("long *a*" in *face*), short in *met*.

I   "   "   " *marine*, short in *pin*.

O   "   "   " *go*, short in *home*, *whole* (as generally pronounced in the northern States).

U   as long in *rule* (oo in *fool*), short in *full* (oo in *good*). *U* as in *union*, *pure*, &c.; to be written yu.

Ɪ   as in *all* (aw, as in *bawl*, *taught*).

Ȧ   "   " *fat*.

Y   "   " *but* (o in *love*, oo in *blood*).

AI   "   " *aisle* ("long *i*" in *pine*).

AU   as ow in *now*, ou in *loud*.

The distinction of long and short vowels to be noted, as far as possible, by the division into syllables, joining a following consonant to a short vowel, and leaving the vowel open if long. Where this is insufficient, or where greater distinctness is desirable, a horizontal mark above, to indicate a long vowel, a curved mark a short one, thus: ā, ă, à, ĕ, &c. A nasal syllable, like those found so commonly in French, to be marked by an index, n, at the upper right-hand corner of the vowel; thus oⁿ, aⁿ, eⁿ, uⁿ, will represent the sounds of the French on, an or en, in, and un, respectively.

CONSONANTS.

B   as in English *blab*.

C   not to be used excepting in the compound *ch*; write *k* for the hard sound, *s* for the soft.

D   as in English *did*.

F   "   "   " *fife*.

G   "   "   " *gig*, never for the soft sound, as in *ginger*; for this use always *j*.

H   as in English *how*, *hoe*, *handle*.

J   "   "   " *judge*.

K   "   "   " *kick*.

L   as in English *lull*.
M   " " " *mimic*.
N   " " " *noon*.
P   " " " *pipe*.
Q   not to be used : for *qu* write *kw*.
R   as in English *rear*.
S   " " " *sauce*.
T   " " " *tight*.
V   " " " *vow*.
W   " " " *wayward*.
X   not to be used : write *ks* or *gz*, according to the sound, in *wax*, *example*.
Y   as in English *you*, *year*.
Z   " " " *zeal*, *buzz*.
R̃   as *ng* in English, *singing*.
SH   as in English *shall*, *shoe*.
ZH   as *z* in *azure*, *s* in *fusion*.
CH   as in English *church*.
TH   " " " *thin*, *truth*.
DH   as *th* in *the*, *with*.
KH   a surd guttural aspirate, the German *ch* in *ach*, *loch*, *buch*, and sometimes approaching that in *ich*, *recht*, *bücher*.
GH   a sonant guttural aspirate (Arabic *ghain*); other compounds, like the clucks occurring in Chinook, &c., to be represented by *kl*, *thl*, *tlk*, &c., according to their analysis.

COMPARATIVE VOCABULARY.

ENGLISH. *Name of tribe.*	SPANISH. *Nombre de la tribu.*
1 man	1 hombre
2 woman	2 mujer
3 boy	3 muchacho
4 girl	4 muchacha
5 infant	5 niño ó niña.
6 my father (said by son)	6 mi padre (dice el hijo)
7 my father (said by daughter)	7 mi padre (dice la hija)
8 my mother (said by son)	8 mi madre (dice el hijo)
9 my mother (said by daughter)	9 mi madre (dice la hija)
10 my husband	10 mi marido
11 my wife	11 mi esposa
12 my son (said by father)	12 mi hijo (dice el padre)
13 my son (said by mother)	13 mi hijo (dice la madre)
14 my daughter (said by father)	14 mi hija (dice el padre)
15 my daughter (said by mother)	15 mi hija (dice la madre)
16 my elder brother	16 mi hermano mayor
17 my younger brother	17 mi hermano menor
18 my elder sister	18 mi hermana mayor
19 my younger sister	19 mi hermana menor
20 an Indian	20 Indio
21 people	21 gente
22 head	22 cabeza
23 hair	23 pelo
24 face	24 cara
25 forehead	25 frente
26 ear	26 oreja
27 eye	27 ojo
28 nose	28 nariz
29 mouth	29 boca

COMPARATIVE VOCABULARY.

FRENCH.	LATIN.
Nom de la tribu.	*Nomen nationis.*
1 homme	1 vir, homo
2 femme	2 mulier
3 garçou	3 puer
4 fille	4 puella
5 enfant	5 infans
6 mon père (dit le fils)	6 pater meus (dicit filius)
7 mon père (dit la fille)	7 pater meus (dicit filia)
8 ma mère (dit le fils)	8 mater mea (dicit filius)
9 ma mère (dit la fille)	9 mater mea (dicit filia)
10 mon mari	10 sponsus meus
11 mon épouse	11 uxor mea
12 mon fils (dit le père)	12 filius meus (dicit pater)
13 mon fils (dit la mère)	13 filius meus (dicit mater)
14 ma fille (dit le père)	14 filia mea (dicit pater)
15 ma fille (dit la mère)	15 filia mea (dicit mater)
16 mon frère aîné	16 frater meus natu major
17 mon frère cadet	17 frater meus natu minor
18 ma sœur aînée	18 soror mea natu major
19 ma sœur cadette	19 soror mea natu minor
20 sauvage	20 Indus
21 peuple	21 populus
22 tête	22 caput
23 cheveux	23 crinis
24 figure	24 facies
25 front	25 frons
26 oreille	26 auris
27 œil	27 oculus
28 nez	28 nasus
29 bouche	29 os

ENGLISH.		SPANISH.	
Name of tribe.		*Nombre de la tribu.*	
30	tongue	30	lengua
31	teeth	31	dientes
32	beard	32	barba
33	neck	33	cuello
34	arm	34	brazo
35	hand	35	mano
36	fingers	36	dedos
37	thumb	37	dedo pulgar
38	nails	38	uñas
39	body	39	cuerpo
40	chest	40	pecho
41	belly	41	barriga
42	female breasts	42	pechos de mujer
43	leg	43	pierna
44	foot	44	pié
45	toes	45	dedos del pié
46	bone	46	hueso
47	heart	47	corazon
48	blood	48	sangre
49	town, village	49	pueblo, villa, aldea
50	chief	50	jefe
51	warrior	51	guerrero
52	friend	52	amigo
53	house	53	casa
54	skin lodge	54	casa de cueros
55	kettle	55	caldera
56	bow	56	arco
57	arrow	57	flecha
58	axe, hatchet	58	hacha
59	knife	59	cuchillo
60	canoe	60	canoa
61	moccasins	61	zapatos Indios
62	pipe	62	pipa

FRENCH.		LATIN.	
Nom de la tribu.		*Nomen gentium.*	
30	langue	30	lingua
31	dents	31	dentes
32	barbe	32	barba
33	cou	33	collis
34	bras	34	brachium
35	main	35	manus
36	doigts	36	digiti
37	pouce	37	digitus pollex
38	ongles	38	ungues
39	corps	39	corpus
40	poitrine	40	sternum
41	ventre	41	venter
42	mamelles	42	ubera
43	jambe	43	crus
44	pied	44	pes
45	doigts du pied	45	digiti pedis
46	os	46	os
47	cœur	47	cor
48	sang	48	sanguis
49	bourg, village	49	oppidum, pagus
50	capitaine	50	dux
51	guerrier	51	miles
52	ami	52	amicus
53	maison	53	domus
54	loge de peaux	54	tentorium e pellibus
55	chaudière	55	lebes
56	arc	56	arcus
57	flèche	57	sagitta
58	hache	58	ascia
59	couteau	59	culter
60	canot	60	scapha Indica
61	soubers de sauvage	61	calceamenta Indica
62	pipe	62	tubus nicotianus

	ENGLISH.		SPANISH.
	Name of tribe		*Nombre de la tribu*
63	tobacco	63	tabaco
64	sky	64	cielo
65	sun	65	sol
66	moon	66	luna
67	star	67	estrella
68	day	68	dia
69	night	69	noche
70	morning	70	mañana
71	evening	71	tarde
72	spring	72	primavera
73	summer	73	verano
74	autumn	74	otoño
75	winter	75	invierno
76	wind	76	viento
77	thunder	77	trueno
78	lightning	78	relámpago
79	rain	79	lluvia
80	snow	80	nieve
81	fire	81	fuego
82	water	82	agua
83	ice	83	hielo
84	earth, land	84	tierra
85	sea	85	mar
86	river	86	rio
87	lake	87	lago
88	valley	88	valle
89	prairie	89	llano
90	hill, mountain	90	cerro, montaña
91	island	91	isla
92	stone, rock	92	piedra, roca
93	salt	93	sal
94	iron	94	hierro
95	forest	95	bosque, selva

	FRENCH.		LATIN.
	Nom de la tribu.		*Nomen nationis.*
63	tabac	63	nicotianum
64	ciel	64	cœlum
65	sol	65	sol
66	lune	66	luna
67	étoile	67	stella
68	jour	68	dies
69	nuit	69	nox
70	matin	70	tempus matutinum
71	soir	71	vesper
72	printemps	72	ver
73	été	73	æstas
74	automne	74	autumnus
75	hiver	75	hibernus
76	vent	76	ventus
77	tonnerre	77	tonitru
78	éclair	78	fulgur
79	pluie	79	pluviam
80	neige	80	nix
81	feu	81	ignis
82	eau	82	aqua
83	glace	83	glacies
84	terre	84	terra
85	mer	85	mar
86	fleuve, rivière	86	flumen
87	lac	87	lacus
88	vallée	88	vallis
89	prairie	89	pratum
90	côte, montagne	90	collis, mons
91	île	91	insula
92	pierre, roche	92	petra, saxum
93	sel	93	sal
94	fer	94	ferrum
95	forêt	95	sylva

	ENGLISH. *Name of tribe.*		SPANISH. *Nombre de la tribu.*
96	tree	96	árbol
97	wood	97	madera
98	leaf	98	hoja
99	bark	99	corteza
100	grass	100	zacate
101	pine	101	pino
102	maize	102	maiz
103	squash	103	calabaza
104	flesh, meat	104	carne
105	dog	105	perro
106	buffalo	106	*bisonte, bufalo
107	bear	107	oso
108	wolf	108	lobo
109	fox	109	zorra
110	deer	110	ciervo
111	elk	111	
112	beaver	112	castor
113	rabbit, hare	113	conejo
114	tortoise	114	tortuga
115	horse	115	caballo
116	fly	116	mosca
117	mosquito	117	mosquito
118	snake	118	culebra, serpiente
119	rattlesnake	119	culebra de cascabel
120	bird	120	ave
121	egg	121	huevo
122	feathers	122	plumas
123	wings	123	alas
124	goose	124	ganso
125	duck (mallard)	125	pato
126	turkey	126	pavo, guanajo
127	pigeon	127	pichon
128	fish	128	pez

FRENCH.		LATIN.	
Nom de la tribu.		*Nomen antiquum.*	
96	arbre	96	arbor
97	bois	97	lignum
98	feuille	98	folium
99	écorce	99	cortex
100	herbe	100	herba
101	pin	101	pinus
102	maïs	102	zea mais
103	citrouille	103	cucurbitus
104	chair	104	caro
105	chien	105	canis
106	buffle	106	bison, bos americanus
107	ours	107	ursus
108	loup	108	lupus
109	renard	109	vulpes
110	cerf	110	cervus
111	élan	111	cervus canadensis
112	castor	112	castor
113	lapin, lièvre	113	lepus
114	tortue	114	testudo
115	cheval	115	equus
116	mouche	116	musca
117	maringouin	117	culex
118	serpent	118	serpens
119	serpent à sonnettes	119	crotalus
120	oiseau	120	avis
121	œuf	121	ovum
122	plumes	122	plumæ
123	aile	123	ala
124	oie	124	anser
125	canard	125	anas boschas
126	dindon	126	pavo
127	tourte	127	columba
128	poisson	128	piscis

	ENGLISH. Name of tribe.		SPANISH. Nombre de la tribu.
129	salmon	129	salmon
130	sturgeon	130	esturion
131	name	131	nombre
132	white	132	blanco
133	black	133	negro
134	red	134	colorado
135	light blue	135	azul celeste
136	yellow	136	amarillo
137	light green	137	verde
138	great, large	138	grande
139	small, little	139	pequeño
140	strong	140	fuerte
141	old	141	viejo
142	young	142	jóven
143	good	143	bueno
144	bad	144	malo
145	dead	145	muerto
146	alive	146	vivo
147	cold	147	frio
148	warm, hot	148	caliente
149	I	149	yo
150	thou	150	tú
151	he	151	él
152	we	152	nosotros
153	ye	153	vosotros
154	they	154	ellos
155	this	155	esto
156	that	156	aquel
157	all	157	todo, todos
158	many, much	158	mucho, muchos
159	who	159	quien
160	far	160	lejos
161	near	161	cerca de

	FRENCH.			LATIN.	
	Nom de la tribu.	:		*Nomen nationis.*	
129	saumon		129	salmo	
130	esturgeon		130	sturio	
131	nom		131	nomen	
132	blanc		132	albus	
133	noir		133	niger	
134	rouge		134	rubrum	
135	bleu		135	cœruleum	
136	jaune		136	amarillis	
137	vert		137	viridis	
138	grand		138	magnus	
139	petit		139	parvus	
140	fort		140	fortis	
141	vieux		141	vetus	
142	jeune		142	juvenis	
143	bon		143	bonus	
144	mauvais		144	malus	
145	mort		145	mortuus	
146	vivant		146	vivus	
147	froid		147	frigidus	
148	chaud		148	calidus	
149	je		149	ego	
150	tu		150	tu	
151	il		151	ille	
152	nous		152	nos	
153	vous		153	vos	
154	ils		154	illi	
155	ceci		155	iste	
156	cela		156	ille	
157	tout, tous		157	omnia, totus	
158	beaucoup		158	multus	
159	qui		159	qui	
160	loin		160	longe	
161	près		161	prope	

	ENGLISH. Name of tribe.		SPANISH. Nombre de la tribu.
162	here	162	aqni
163	there	163	allá
164	to-day	164	hoy
165	yesterday	165	ayer
166	to-morrow	166	mañana (el dia de)
167	yes	167	sí
168	no	168	no
169	one	169	uno
170	two	170	dos
171	three	171	tres
172	four	172	cuatro
173	five	173	cinco
174	six	174	seis
175	seven	175	siete
176	eight	176	ocho
177	nine	177	nueve
178	ten	178	diez
179	eleven	179	once
180	twelve	180	doce
181	twenty	181	veinte
182	thirty	182	treinta
183	forty	183	cuarenta
184	fifty	184	cincuenta
185	sixty	185	sesenta
186	seventy	186	setenta
187	eighty	187	ochenta
188	ninety	188	noventa
189	one hundred	189	ciento
190	one thousand	190	mil
191	to eat	191	comer
192	to drink	192	beber
193	to run	193	correr
194	to dance	194	bailar

FRENCH.		LATIN.	
Nom de la tribu.		*Nomen nationis.*	
162	ici	162	hic
163	là	163	illuc
164	aujourd'hui	164	hodie
165	hier	165	heri
166	demain	166	cras
167	oui	167	ita
168	non	168	minime
169	un	169	unus
170	deux	170	duo
171	trois	171	tres
172	quatre	172	quatuor
173	cinq	173	quinque
174	six	174	sex
175	sept	175	septem
176	huit	176	octo
177	neuf	177	novem
178	dix	178	decem
179	onze	179	undecim
180	douze	180	duodecim
181	vingt	181	viginti
182	trente	182	triginta
183	quarante	183	quadraginta
184	cinquante	184	quinquaginta
185	soixante	185	sexaginta
186	soixante-dix	186	septuaginta
187	quatre-vingts	187	octoginta
188	quatre-vingt-dix	188	nonaginta
189	cent	189	centum
190	mille	190	mille
191	manger	191	edere
192	boire	192	bibere
193	courir	193	currere
194	danser	194	saltare

ENGLISH.	SPANISH.
Name of tribe.	*Nombre de la tribu.*
195 to sing	195 cantar
196 to sleep	196 dormir
197 to speak	197 hablar
198 to see	198 ver
199 to love	199 amar
200 to kill	200 matar
201 to sit	201 sentarse
202 to stand	202 estar en pie
203 to go	203 ir
204 to come	204 venir
205 to walk	205 andar
206 to work	206 trabajar
207 to steal	207 robar
208 to lie	208 mentir
209 to give	209 dar
210 to laugh	210 reir
211 to cry	211 gritar

	FRENCH.		LATIN.
	Nom de la tribu.		*Nomen nationis.*
195	chanter	195	cantare
196	dormir	196	dormire
197	parler	197	loqui
198	voir	198	videre
199	aimer	199	amare
200	tuer	200	cadere
201	s'asseoir	201	sedere
202	se tenir debout	202	stare
203	aller	203	ire
204	venir	204	venire
205	marcher	205	ambulare
206	travailler	206	operari
207	voler	207	furare
208	mentir	208	mentiri
209	donner	209	dare
210	rire	210	ridere
211	crier	211	clamare

INSTRUCTIONS

RELATIVE TO THE

ETHNOLOGY AND PHILOLOGY OF AMERICA.

APPENDIX A.

PHYSICAL CHARACTER OF THE INDIAN RACES.

INVESTIGATIONS are now being made into the physical character of the soldiers composing the armies of the United States, embracing a large number of measurements of different parts of the body, designed to ascertain the effect of climate, locality, and mode of life upon men, the average size and proportions of troops of the United States as compared with those of foreign countries, and those of the different States as compared with each other.

In connection with this inquiry it is deemed a matter of interest to extend the examination to the Indian tribes of America, and to ascertain the proportions of the aboriginal races as compared with those of European descent, and also the effects of different food, climate, and mode of life upon the various tribes of the former.

The measurements selected for this purpose are, for various reasons, limited to a smaller number than in the case of the army, and with the exception of that of weight, which as being variable is of the least consequence, are such as can be taken with a tape-measure. They should be made with great care in feet, inches, and tenths of an inch.

Persons familiar with the Indians are aware that a great difference exists in the complexion, not merely of individuals, but of tribes. In some cases that peculiar reddish tinge of the skin which has given to the race the name of "Red" or "Copper-colored Men" is predominant and marked; in others a light brown is the more common; again, a yellowish or somewhat orange hue exhibits itself; and, finally, some approach nearly to black. Among the lighter colored the red often shows in the

cheek. Nor are these diversities due altogether to climate or
exposure. There seem to be well authenticated instances in
which food also influences complexion. Thus it is said that
among the Chepewyan tribes of British America, the Cariboo or
Reindeer eaters are much darker than the cognate tribes who
live on fish, and this, too, although they inhabit a far northern
latitude. The texture of the skin is a noticeable feature. That of
the younger Indians, where it can be perceived through the dirt,
is usually exceedingly soft and delicate, but becomes wrinkled
with middle age. An important difference in the color of the
hair also occasionally shows itself. For instance, the Indians of
the Nooksahk tribe, in the neighborhood of Mount Baker, Washington Territory, have often light-brown and even flaxen hair in
youth, which, however, grows dark with age, and yet their blood
is unmixed. When neglected and exposed to the sun the hair
becomes of a rusty hue, and like that of whites loses its gloss.
Among some of the Pueblo tribes of New Mexico albinos are
not uncommon. Hazel eyes are frequent among the Indians of
the lower Klamath.

Particular information should be given as to their food, whether
consisting of game, fish, maize, roots, &c., and even as to the
kinds of either, whether of buffalo, elk, deer, or cariboo, of salmon
or other varieties of river fish, or of the various animal productions of the sea, such as the whale, walrus, seals, &c., as among
the Esquimaux and some of the Northwest Coast Indians.

Their mode of life will, of course, influence the development
of the form. Among the tribes who live almost altogether on
horseback, or in canoes, we may expect to see the legs comparatively small, while in the latter the arms will be proportionately
large. Among the mountain tribes, on the other hand, the legs
will be more muscular and the chest expanded. As a general
rule their limbs are rounded, and the separate muscles are not
developed as in the white and black races. As to this, observations are requested.

The age of Indians it is very difficult, in most cases impossible,
to ascertain, as they keep no record even in memory. An esti-
mate founded on careful observation will, however, afford a
reasonable approximation. Sometimes a reference to a known
event as having occurred when they were of the size of some
young boy will afford a guide. As the men usually marry young,

the age of their families furnishes often another. A great age, notwithstanding apparent decrepitude, is very rarely attained, especially by the male sex.

In the case of mixed breeds it is by all means desirable to ascertain and state whether either one or both parents were themselves mixed, and, if so, to what degree. Any observations on the comparative physical development, health, and length of life among the mixed broods will be very gladly received.

Where the inquiry is made by medical men, other points will naturally suggest themselves. Among them, it will be well to ascertain the number of regular pulsations and respirations per minute.

It is hardly necessary to add that these measurements should be confined to adult males. Observations on boys who have not attained their growth would have no value.

PARTICULARS OF INQUIRY.

In order to avoid the necessity of transcribing the questions, references may be made to the numbers and letters. Separate tables in quarto have been prepared, and will be furnished on application to the Smithsonian Institution.

1. Name of Indian.
2. Name of tribe.
3. If of mixed blood, in what proportion?
4. Country occupied by tribe.
5. Mode of subsistence, whether by hunting, fishing, &c. Habits, whether used to riding, foot, or canoe travel.
6. Articles of usual food.
7. Age (by estimation) between 20 and 30, 30 and 40, &c.
8. State of general health.
9. Weight in lbs. and half lbs.
10. General complexion, whether reddish, brown, yellowish, or black.

11. Hair, color of.

12. Eyes, color of.
    a. Whether oblique or not.
    b. Distance between outer angles }
        over root of nose.

13. Teeth.
    a. How many are lost?
    b. Are they much ground down }
        by hard food?
    c. Do the opposing incisor teeth }
        of the two jaws rest on each }
        other, do they overlap?

14. Entire height without shoes.

15. Head.
    a. Largest circumference around.
    b. Distance between orifices of }
        ears over top of head.
    c. Distance from root of nose over }
        top of the head to base of }
        skull.

16. Arm.
    a. Length outside from point of }
        shoulder cap to tip of mid- }
        dle finger.
    b. Length from same to point of }
        elbow when bent.
    c. Length from point of elbow to }
        lower end of ulna.
    d. Length from lower end of ulna }
        to tip of middle finger.
    e. Largest girth of arm.
    f. Largest girth of forearm.
    g. Largest girth of hand.

17. Distance from upper centre of breast }
    bone to end of middle finger, arm }
    extended.

18. Breadth of shoulders behind.

19. Girth of neck.

20. Girth of chest around nipples.
    a. With full inspiration.
    b. After expiration.
21. Girth of waist.
22. Girth around hips on level with the } head of the thigh bones.

23. Leg.
    a. Height from ground to top of } hip-bone, outside.
    b. Height to knee-joint outside.
    c. Height to crotch inside.
    d. Largest girth of thigh.
    e. Largest girth of leg.

24. Foot.
    a. Length from tip of great toe } to extremity of heel.
    b. Girth of instep.
    c. Girth around heel and instep.

INSTRUCTIONS

RELATIVE TO THE

ETHNOLOGY AND PHILOLOGY OF AMERICA.

APPENDIX B.

NUMERAL SYSTEMS.

IN the original circular of "Instructions" allusion was made to the fact that some of the Indian tribes use different sets of numerals, or rather modifications of the numerals, as applied to different objects. This fact, in connection with the various serial systems upon which their enumeration is based, presents a subject worthy of particular inquiry, the more especially as the same singularity exists among other distant and distinct barbarous nations.

Mr. Gallatin in his "Notes on the Semi-Civilized Nations of Mexico," &c., published in the Transactions of the American Ethnological Society (vol. II. p. 54, et seq.), says: "Another peculiarity of the Mexican and Maya, and of which traces may be seen in other languages of the same group, is the alteration which the numerals undergo according to the nature of the object to be counted. The distinctions are not always easy to be understood; and the objects of the same class, that is to say in counting which the same altered numeral is used, are apparently of the same incongruous nature. Those stated by Father Alonzo de Mollas for the Mexican language, are as follows:—

1	ce, cem	6	chica-ce
2	ome	7	chic-ome
3	yey	8	chic-uey
4	naui	9	chicu-naui
5	macuilli	10	mat-lactli
		20	cem-ponalli "

I have excerpted only the first ten numerals and the word for twenty from Mr. Gallatin's Table A. He proceeds:—

"The numerals as laid down in Table A. are used in counting animated beings, mantas, mats, paper, tortillas, ropes, skins, canoes, cycles, knives, and candles; but in counting several of them, the word *pilli* and sometimes *quimilli*, is substituted for *poualli* (20).

"The syllable *tetl* is added to the numerals, and these lose their last syllable (*mallactetl* for *mallacti*, *cem-poualletl* for *cem-poualli*) when counting fowls, eggs, cocoa, jars, frijoles, fruits, roots, rolls, or round things.

"The word *pantli* is added to the numeral when speaking of ridges made by the plough, of walls, files of men, and of other things arranged in length.

"*Tlementli* is added to the numeral when speaking of speeches, dishes, bags, shields, or when a thing is doubled above another, or when speaking of things differing one from the other."

No reference to such a system is to be found in the Grammatical sketch of the Havz, translated by Mr. Buckingham Smith (No. III of Shea's Linguistics); in the Nevome Grammar (ibid. No. V), the maison of Father Arroyo (ib. No. IV), or Father Sitjar's vocabulary of the San Antonio (ib. No. VII), the only extended works at present accessible on the languages of Sonora and California, but it is very possible that it may exist there and have escaped notice.

In Father Pandosy's Grammar of the Yakama, a Sahaptin language of Washington Territory (Shea's Linguistics, No. V), the numerals are not specially referred to; but in the accompanying dictionary *metal* is given for three, *metao*, three persons; *pinepl* for four, *pinapo* four persons; *paral* five, *par-nao*, five persons, and other numerals are given in duplicate or triplicate without explanation.

Father Mengarini, in his Grammar of the Selish, or Flathead of the Rocky Mountains (Shea, No. II.), says of the cardinal numbers, "they are duplex, one set relating to things, the other to persons, thus:—"

Relating to things.	*Relating to persons.*
1 nko	schnaked
2 esèl	chetèl
3 chèlès	ch'chèlès
4 mús	ch'músms
5 sll	ch'sllsil
6 tackan	ch'tackan
7 sispel	ch'sispel
8 hèhènem	ch'hèhènem
9 ganút	ch'gannt
10 open	ch'open

Similar changes exist in other dialects of the Selish, of which the following from the Nisqually will serve as an instance:—

Applied to men.	*Applied to money.*
1 dut-cho	che-élts
2 salo	sla-élts
3 klekhw	kle-hwélts
4 bós	bós-élts
5 tsa-lats	tslat-sélts
6 dze-lá-chl	dzlatch-élts
7 tsóks	tsok-sélts
8 l'ká-chí	l'ka-chl-élts
9 hwul	hwul-élts
10 pa-duts	pa-dats-élts
20 sa-lá-chl	

Zeisberger in his "Grammar of the Language of the Lenni-Lenape, or Delaware Indians" (Trans. Am. Phil. Soc., N. S., vol. iii), gives the list of numerals, without stating its application, as follows:—

1	nguttl	6	guttasch
2	nischa	7	nischasch
3	nacha	8	chasch
4	newo	9	peachkouk
5	palenach	10	tellen

And then adds the following, used in respect to inanimate objects, as towns, rivers, houses, &c.

Mawat, *ngutti*, one, only one, and in the plural, *nischenol*, two, *nachenol*, three, &c., concerning which he observes, "When men, animals, or other things are spoken of, which among the

Indians are considered as belonging to the animated class of beings, they say: *mauchsa, moyauchsa*, one person, or a person, or living being. It is truly incorrect to say *ngutti lenno*, a man. And in the plural, *nischowak lennowak*, two men, &c.

All and *ak*, the terminations of these last in the plural, are respectively applied, the former to inanimate, the latter to animate objects. But as exceptions, it is stated that among nouns, trees and the larger plants are considered animate, while fishes take the inanimate termination. It is thus evident that a similar idea has governed the form of the numeral adjective in the Delaware and the Mexican.

Other examples among the North American languages might be cited, but the above are sufficient to indicate the object of inquiry. The system appears, however, not to have been universal, as, according to Dr. Wilson, there is no distinction of numerals in the Seneca or other Iroquois languages.

Singularly enough, the same idea prevails in the numerals of other and far distant races, of which a few specimens may be useful.

The Hon. John Pickering, in "Memoirs of the American Academy," N. S., vol. II, gives an account of the language and inhabitants of Tobi, or Lord North's Island, in the Indian Archipelago, derived from an American seaman, Horace Holden, who spent two years upon it. This island is situated about lat. 3° 5′ north and lon. 131° 4′ east, and is of very small extent and sparsely inhabited. The different forms of the digits are thus given in the accompanying vocabulary:—

General cardinals.	For cocoanuts.	For fish.
1	yat	su	simül
2	guh-lu	guó	gwimül
3	ya	sarú	srimül
4	van	vao	vamül
5	ni	limó	nimül
6	wör	waru	wawrimül
7	vish	vishu	vishi-emül
8	wawr	ilu (?)	wawrimul
9	iló	(wauling)	tnimal
10	se or sek	sek	sek

He adds, however, that in counting out fish, they proceed by pairs or couples, as, two, four, six, &c.

In counting *fish hooks*, they use still a different set of numerals, which were not recollected. It would appear further that stones, birds, and days were counted by the same numerals as cocoanuts, and men and women by those employed to enumerate fish.

Mr. Hale, in the "Ethnography, &c., of the U. S. Exploring Expedition," copies Holden's vocabulary, which is also appended to a narrative of his captivity, published at Boston.

Dr. L. H. Gulick, in his notes on the Grammar of the Ponape dialect (12mo. Honolulu, 1858, pp. 39), states that "the enumeration of all objects is alike as far as *nine*, after which there is a singular variety." The difference is in—

"I. The mode of counting all animated objects, and all kinds of sticks and timbers, and everything that to a native is connected in idea with separate sticks, as trees, canoes, &c.

"II. The enumeration of yams, taro, and a few of the most costly articles.

"III. The numbering of cocoanuts, bread-fruits, eggs, shells, stones, &c., in fact, probably, of all common, least valued objects, not included under the first head."

Examples are given, not necessary to repeat here, as also of peculiarities in the numerative particles.

The Island of Ponape, P'sanopa, or, as written by Mr. Hale, Bonabe, is one of the central islands of Micronesia. That gentleman gives also a vocabulary of the language of Tapoteoua, in the Kingsmill group, one of the most eastern, and separated from Tobi by 2600 miles. Speaking of the numerals, he says that the natives furnished the expedition with several sets or classes, which he conjectured were used in counting objects of different kinds, though he had no means of obtaining from them any explanation. There were five of them in all, and all given in the digits, or from one to ten.—Eth. of Ex. Exp. p. 440.

Leaving Micronesia for Polynesia, Mr. Hale states that some of the terms for the higher numbers are only used in counting particular articles. For *four*, the Hawaiians, for instance, have two terms, *ha* and *tanna*. For forty, they have *tanahá, iaio*, and *ta'au*. The first of these, *tanahá*, is the general term; *iaio* is used in counting pieces of *tapa* (native cloth), and *ta'au* in counting fish. (Ib. p. 250.)

It is remarkable that thus, in Tobi and Tapoteoua, the distinction should extend to all the digits; and in Ponape, which

Is between the two, and Hawaii, distant 3500 miles, it should be confined to the higher numbers.

The last example here presented is from Bowen's Yoruba Dictionary, in the 10th vol. Smithsonian Contributions. In this, an African Language, traces of the same system also appear. Thus in ordinary counting the first vowel is short, while among what the author terms "cardinals of price," up to forty, the vowel is long; thus *okay*, one, *edil*, two; *ólay*, *edil*. The reason given for this is that the latter are contractions of *owó-kay*, *owó-edil*, i. e. one cowrie, two cowries, &c.

It thus appears that this peculiar arithmetic is of wide distribution, and by no means confined to a single or even to cognate races. A more perfect knowledge of barbarian languages would probably show its still greater extension. In what process of the human mind it has its origin, and the reasons for the singular collocation of objects which different tribes embrace in the several forms of the numerals, are questions of curious speculation.

The division of objects into animate and inanimate, or, as they have been termed by other writers, noble and ignoble, is a well-known feature in several of the languages of North America. Mr. Howse states that the Cree and Chippeway (Ojibwa) nouns are divisible into two classes, animate and inanimate, analogous to gender in European languages, but that many inanimate nouns, from possessing some real or imaginary excellence, are personified as animates. Perhaps a clue to this may be found in the pantheism, or rather pan-demonism of the Indian mythology. The Indians of Oregon, for example, believe that not only all animals were once people possessed of supernatural powers, or magicians, but that prominent mountains, isolated rocks, very old trees, and other remarkable objects, were so likewise, a belief which, in fact, seems to have characterized the superstitions of all the tribes of the continent. But, though this might account for a simple division into animate and inanimate, embracing all such objects, it would not explain the multiplicity of forms exhibited in some of the examples above given. The disposition to particularize, and the want of generic terms among barbarous races, may have had some connection with this division, for since to adopt a different system of counting every object would be impossible, the simple desire to be specific may have led to an anomalous form of classification.

The second object in this investigation is to ascertain the series of numbers upon which enumeration is based among different tribes. The most natural, and, among barbarous nations, most common, is the quinary system, or that by fives, corresponding with the fingers of one hand. In this the first five digits are simple, that is to say, are all different ; the second form compounds or modifications of these first, as will be seen by referring back to the example given of the Mexican. In many cases, however, it has happened that, in the lapse of time, new words have been adopted for a portion, while the old have become obsolete, or appear only occasionally in combination. In a number of vocabularies examined, it would appear that the numbers 7 and 8 most frequently retain the compound form, and 10 has oftenest changed. The 7 and 8 usually contain the elements of the words 2 and 3, as representing the 2d and 3d fingers on the second hand. Nine is frequently "one less than ten."

Probably in almost all these languages the quinary system was the oldest, and the decimal, where it now exists, has been of subsequent introduction, or rather growth. In the Chinook, for example, the names of the digits are all simple with the exception of that for seven. Thus *makst* two, *sini-makst* seven, *sini* being, perhaps, an obsolete form of five. These obsolete forms are sometimes revealed in the numeral ten and its compounds and multiples. Thus the simple digit ten may have one name, while in eleven=10+1, or twenty=2×10, the word will be entirely different. In the Napa, of California, *hopen* signifies two, and *ma-ha-ish* ten, but twenty is *hopi-hoi*, the other multiples retaining the syllable *hoi* up to one hundred, which is *ma-ha-ish soi*, the h being changed to s for euphony.

Twenty is, in some languages, a translation of *two tens*, in others a distinct word exists, and this is in many the name for bead, body, or person, as in the Opata, *seris dosme* (literally one person), signifying, of course, all the fingers and toes of one person. In the Nisqually the word for twenty, *s'ha-lat-chl*, means literally the fingers and toes. As to the other multiples of ten, they are usually expressed by the literal translation of 8×10, 4×10, &c. But in the Opata and kindred dialects this form occurs, 20, *seris dosme*; 30, *seris dosme macoi tareua*, i. e. ten more than one person; 40, *wodem dosme*, or two twenties; 50,

wodun dosme macoi tarewa; 60, beidum dosme, three twenties, &c.

A good many anomalous forms occur, unnecessary to repeat
here, as, for instance, 2×4 for 8, 3×8 for six.

Besides the quinary and decimal series, the binary and vigin-
tesimal are supposed to be represented.

A sufficient number of extended vocabularies of numerals have
not been obtained to admit of a thorough examination and comparison of the different series in use, and the following table has,
therefore, been prepared, which will enable the collector to com-
bine both subjects of inquiry in one, the figures having been
selected in reference to the latter, and the arrangement in parallel
columns to the former. These are headed "Simple Cardinals,"
"Personal Cardinals," and "Cardinals of Value," merely as a
guide, and not as indicating that they will in all cases convey
the true idea. It is desired that as careful inquiry as possible
should be made into the facts in each one, and that the objects
included in the separate classes be enumerated. It is probable
that in some languages other columns must be added.

Very few tribes, it will be found, count beyond 100, while some
of the more ignorant have no numbers beyond five. It is desirable in all cases, if possible, to ascertain the meaning of the larger
collective numbers, as 10, 20, and 100, and another point of inquiry may be the names of the different fingers, especially of the
thumb, thus:—

Little finger.
Ring finger.
Middle finger
Fore-finger.
Thumb.

www.ingramcontent.com/pod-product-compliance
Lightning Source LLC
Chambersburg PA
CBHW020254290326
41930CB00039B/1379